General editor: Graham Handl

Brodie's Notes on Sean O'Casey's
Juno and the Paycock

W. S. Bunnell

150th YEAR
M
MACMILLAN

First published 1978 by Pan Books Ltd

This revised edition published 1993 by
THE MACMILLAN PRESS LTD
Houndmills, Basingstoke, Hampshire RG21 2XS
and London
Companies and representatives
throughout the world

ISBN 0-333-58163-6

Typeset by Footnote Graphics, Warminster, Wiltshire
Printed in Great Britain by
Cox & Wyman Ltd, Reading

Contents

Preface

The intention throughout this study aid is to stimulate and guide, to encourage your involvement in the book, and to develop informed responses and a sure understanding of the main details.

Brodie's Notes provide a clear outline of the play or novel's plot, followed by act, scene, or chapter summaries and/or commentaries. These are designed to emphasize the most important literary and factual details. Poems, stories or nonfiction texts combine brief summary with critical commentary on individual aspects or common features of the genre being examined. Textual notes define what is difficult or obscure and emphasize literary qualities. Revision questions are set at appropriate points to test your ability to appreciate the prescribed book and to write accurately and relevantly about it.

In addition, each of these Notes includes a critical appreciation of the author's art. This covers such major elements as characterization, style, structure, setting and themes. Poems are examined technically – rhyme, rhythm, for instance. In fact, any important aspect of the prescribed work will be evaluated. The aim is to send you back to the text you are studying.

Each study aid concludes with a series of general questions which require a detailed knowledge of the book: some of these questions may invite comparison with other books, some will be suitable for coursework exercises, and some could be adapted to work you are doing on another book or books. Each study aid has been adapted to meet the needs of the current examination requirements. They provide a basic, individual and imaginative response to the work being studied, and it is hoped that they will stimulate you to acquire disciplined reading habits and critical fluency.

Graham Handley 1990

The close reading of the play is the student's primary task; try to see it performed if possible. These Notes are designed to increase the understanding and appreciation of the play – they in no way provide a substitute for familiarity with it.

The plays that are most valuable as background to the study of *Juno and the Paycock* are those written during the same period and with a similar artistic intention: *The Shadow of a Gunman* and *The Plough and the Stars*. *The Silver Tassie* is also concerned with war, although not in an Irish setting. Of the later plays, O'Casey considered *Cock-a-doodle-Dandy* to be his best work. *Red Roses for Me* contains some illuminating autobiographical elements. *Within the Gates* is an example of O'Casey's dramatic experiment. These are all available in the *Collected Plays*, published in four volumes (Macmillan). They are also available in *The Sean O'Casey Reader*, edited by Brooks Atkinson and published in England by Macmillan (1968). This work also contains a useful selection from the autobiographies. Those covering the period of the early plays are the most relevant: *Drums Under the Windows* and *Inishfallen, Fare Thee Well*.

Page references in these Notes are to the Papermac (Macmillan paperback) edition of *Three Plays by Sean O'Casey*, but as references are also made to individual Acts, the Notes may be used with any edition of the play.

The author and his work

John Casey was born in Dublin on 30 March 1880. He was the youngest of thirteen children, only five of whom survived early childhood. As a young man learning the Irish language he changed his name to Sean O'Cathasaigh; later, when he made his debut as a dramatist, he became Sean O'Casey.

When he was six years old his father died and, already poor, the family was reduced to severe poverty. Sean suffered ill health and weak eyesight. His mother was a Protestant, bringing her son up in her own faith, and through their poverty they were thrown into close contact with their equally poor Catholic neighbours; they had nothing to do with the affluent middle class to which most Protestants belonged.

O'Casey had little formal education; his mother read the Bible to him, and he read second-hand books, memorizing parts of the plays of Shakespeare and Dion Boucicault under the influence of his brother Archie, who was a member of an amateur theatrical group.

A deep and lasting influence in his early life was the Reverend E. M. Griffin, the Rector of the church of St Barnabas. His 'sensitive hand was the first to give the clasp of friendship to the author', O'Casey wrote in later years.

He began work at the age of fourteen in the stockroom of a hardware firm; he occupied various clerical posts and then turned to working as a manual labourer, continuing to do this until he began to write full-time in 1925. During this period he bought and studied second-hand copies of Shakespeare, Goldsmith, Sheridan, Dickens, Balzac, Scott, Ruskin, Byron, Keats and Shelley.

In his early twenties he became an enthusiastic member of the Gaelic League and the Irish Republican Brotherhood. Under the influence of Karl Marx's ideas he gradually formed the conviction that poverty was the great evil to be fought. He identified himself with the suffering of the working class, rather than with the cultural and nationalist ideals that he associated with the middle class. It is this shift of thought that provides the key to many of the political and social ideas expressed in *Juno and the Paycock*. Socialism replaced his religious and nationalist beliefs as the prime mover of his writing. 'I never lost my faith,' he wrote, 'I found it. I found it when Jim Larkin came to Dublin and organized the unskilled workers. I found it in Jim's great socialist motto: "An injury to one is the concern of all." (*Sean O'Casey and his World*, D. Krause, Thames & Hudson.) He was the saviour of Dublin. He put his faith in the people and their need to live a better and fuller life. And that's where I put my faith.'

Jim Larkin was a vital influence on O'Casey. In 1914 O'Casey became secretary to the Irish Citizen Army formed by the trade unions to protect the workers from the brutality of the police. O'Casey actively supported the general strike organized by Larkin, but, significantly, he did not play an active part in the Easter Rising of 1916, the noble failure that became an abiding inspiration for the nationalist movement. He was a socialist first, and a nationalist second. It was this period that provided the background of the later play *Red Roses for Me*, where the hero, who closely resembles the young O'Casey, says, 'Friend, we would that you should live a greater life: we will that all of us shall live a greater life . . . We who have known, and know, the emptiness of life shall know its fullness.'

In his increasing disillusionment with political and military action, O'Casey turned to writing and to the drama. The quality of his courageous determination is revealed in the way he refused to turn aside from his efforts when he suffered the rejection of his early attempts at drama. Indeed, it was a fitting apprenticeship for a dramatist who for most of his life was to have his plays rejected for production in the theatre.

Finally the Abbey Theatre in Dublin accepted *The Shadow of a Gunman* (1922). O'Casey was still working as a labourer.

The Abbey Theatre was filled to capacity for the first time in its history. In 1924 *Juno and the Paycock* was an even bigger success, and its run had to be extended. *The Plough and the Stars* followed in 1926. Some patriots objected to its treatment of the Easter Rising, and riots took place that recalled those that had greeted the production of J. M. Synge's *Playboy of the Western World* in 1907.

Now, as then, W. B. Yeats addressed the turbulent audience: 'You have disgraced yourselves again. Is this to be an ever-recurring celebration of the arrival of Irish genius? Synge first and then O'Casey. The news of the happenings of the past few minutes will go from country to country. Dublin has once more rocked the cradle of genius. From such a scene in this theatre went forth the fame of Synge. Equally the fame of O'Casey is born here tonight. This is his apotheosis.' (*Sean O'Casey and his World*, D. Krause, Thames & Hudson.)

O'Casey, reviled as 'a guttersnipe from the slums', went to London to receive the Hawthornden Prize for *Juno and the Paycock*. He never returned to Dublin to live, although he retained for some time the one-room tenement in which he had written his three great plays.

He had established himself as a playwright of the first order. His plays had placed the Abbey Theatre on a sound financial basis: 'The Abbey owed its recent prosperity to you,' wrote W. B. Yeats. 'If you had not brought us your plays at that moment I doubt if it would now exist.'

He enjoyed London, its atmosphere of freedom, his friendship with the eminent Bernard Shaw and the painter Agustus John. In 1927 he married Eileen Carey, who had played the part of Nora in the London production of *The Plough and the Stars*.

O'Casey's next play, *The Silver Tassie*, was rejected by the Abbey Theatre. It was set against the background of the First World War, and Yeats, in a letter to him, gave this as the reason for its rejection: 'You were interested in the Irish Civil War and at every moment of those plays wrote out of your own amusement with life or your sense of tragedy; you were excited and we all caught your excitement; you were exasperated almost beyond endurance by what you had seen or heard, as a man is by what happens under his window; and you moved us as Swift moved his contemporaries. But you are not interested in the Great War; you never stood on its battlefields ...' (*Modern Judgements: Sean O'Casey*, ed. R. Ayling, Macmillan.) The rejection was to create an enmity between Yeats and O'Casey destined to last until *The Silver Tassie* was eventually performed at the Abbey in 1935, again in an atmosphere of controversy.

The Silver Tassie was presented in London by C. B. Cochran in 1929, but in 1933 Cochran refused to put on *Within the Gates*, an expressionistic play set in Hyde Park in which O'Casey described the stresses of contemporary civilization against a vision of the future. Cochran underlined the dilemma of O'Casey's dramatic development: 'You can't go on writing fine things, Sean, unless they bring some material reward. I suppose you are tired of people advising you to get back to the method of "*Juno*". I wish you would.' O'Casey would not. In spite of poverty, and the responsibility of a wife and three children, he continued to go his own way, belligerent, confident in his own powers and his own approach, believing in life and the betterment of mankind.

He battled with critics, with the Roman Catholic Church – which had always banned his works – the mayor of Boston, Kingsley Martin, the editor of the *New Statesman and Nation*; he attacked Noël Coward and the contemporary English theatre, and demanded, prophetically, an independent National Theatre. In reply to his publisher and friend, Harold Macmillan, who had urged him to be less aggressive in his writing, he wrote: 'My works are, at least, additions to the drama, and defending them, I defend the drama ... Invariably, I have done the things that are not done and left undone the things that are done, and I am not much the worse for it. The theatre is more than good manners. As for "brawling in church", well, Jesus Christ did it before me, and I occasionally follow in His steps.' (*Sean O'Casey and his World*, D. Krause, Thames & Hudson.)

In 1937 he was writing *The Star Turns Red*, which expresses his communist views. He had always looked upon Russia with hope and sympathy, and in this new work the Star of Bethlehem becomes the Red Star. It was first presented at the Unity Theatre in 1940.

His last three comedies, *Cock-a-Doodle-Dandy*, *The Bishop's Bonfire* and *The Drums of Father Ned*, reveal a strange mixture of religious belief, idealism, the glory of mankind and a disillusionment with churches that have manifestly failed to give any sense of joy and freedom in life.

O'Casey was always haunted by the desire for belief. Towards the end of his life he described himself as being 'tired but joyous, praising God for His rightness and the will towards joy in the hearts of men'.

During this period he wrote a number of volumes of unusual and original autobiographies. They do not give an account of his life in ordered chronological sequence, and they often read more like a novel than an autobiography, with the use of third-person narrative. Intense emotional attitudes towards life, and an ecstatic, sometimes undisciplined excitement in words colour the work. The dates of publication are: *I Knock at the Door* (1939), covering roughly the period 1880–90; *Pictures in the Hallway* (1942), covering 1891–1904; *Drums Under the Windows* (1945), covering 1905–16; *Inishfallen, Fare Thee Well* (1949), covering 1916–26; *Rose and Crown* (1952), covering 1926–34; *Sunset and Evening Star* (1954), covering 1934–53 (all originally published by Macmillan, available in paperback by Pan Books).

As old age approached, O'Casey's eyesight, which had troubled him from childhood, worsened. He suffered from bronchitis and a weak heart; then, in 1956, his son Niall, aged twenty, died suddenly. O'Casey was overwhelmed with grief, yet his hope remained undimmed, as he demonstrated in a number of short comedies he wrote at this time.

At the age of eighty-four he still believed in the joy of life, declaring that 'the soft thighs of a young woman' showed the glory of the human body. 'I have found life an enjoyable, enchanting, active and sometimes terrifying experience, and I've enjoyed it completely,' he wrote in a letter.

In his last days he lived in a third-floor flat in a house in Torquay. Family life had always meant much to him, and his marriage had been successful and happy; his wife was at his side when, on 18 September 1964, he died in his sleep following a heart attack.

There had been a great deal in his life of which he might have complained and which would have completely over-whelmed a lesser man. Ill-health, lack of recognition, hostility, poverty had been his lot, yet his achievement was substantial. Had he written nothing but those first three plays that were produced at the Abbey Theatre, his permanent place in the history of the theatre would be secure. It is an indication of his stature that he was able to turn his back on this early success to attempt to develop and exploit new approaches to the drama. The words that he wrote of Shakespeare in *Blasts and Benedictions* could well be applied to himself: 'The world of life was Shakespeare's oyster, and, unlike Auden who found it empty, Shakespeare found it packed with good and grand things. He saw all, heard all, tested many things, felt all the emotions, and he scented the sweet perfumes coming from the hearts of flowers and shrank from the rotten smell that came from war.'

Act summaries, critical commentary, textual notes and revision questions

Act 1

The play opens in a two-room tenancy of a tenement house in Dublin. Breakfast for one is laid on the table. Various objects ranging from books to a labourer's shovel are scattered around. Johnny Boyle, the son, is sitting by the fire. His sister Mary is arranging her hair. The time is early morning. Mrs Juno Boyle, the mother, enters. They are waiting for her husband to return. Mrs Tancred's son has been killed, and his death is reported in the morning paper. Mrs Boyle, who is late for work, becomes increasingly angry at her husband's continued absence, doubtless in the company of his friend Joxer Daly. Johnny, who is out of work and plainly in a disturbed state, was injured during the fighting and a bomb has led to the loss of his arm. Mary, a girl of principle according to her own judgement, is on strike. Jerry Devine, Mary's suitor and a rising figure in the Labour Movement, enters with news of a possible job for 'Captain' Jack Boyle, Juno's husband who is very willingly out of work; Juno complains that, whilst she is killing herself working, he struts about like a peacock all day. At this point he enters, singing. He invites Joxer in, thinking Juno has gone to work. He is wrong. She comes forward and with heavy irony politely invites the unwilling Joxer to stay.

Joxer and Boyle invent a story of a job that they are going after, but Juno is not for one moment deceived. Boyle, having refused the breakfast, is caught by Jerry Devine who first of all reveals that Boyle has just been drinking in Foley's although he has stated to Juno that he has not had a drink for three weeks, and then tells Boyle of possible work. Boyle, faced with the possibility of a job, discovers a pain in his right leg and conjures up a multitude of reasons for not working. Jerry despairingly declares his love to Mary; she is not interested. Plainly another man is involved. When everyone has left Boyle quickly succumbs to the temptation of eating the breakfast Juno has prepared for him. He is interrupted first by a salesman for sewing machines and then by the return of Joxer. Johnny appears at the door asking who is knocking. Joxer refuses to stick his head out of the window to see for fear of a bullet. Johnny is visibly startled when Boyle sees it is a man in a trench coat. Johnny returns to the other room when the man goes away. Boyle and Joxer talk about Mary's books, Jerry, the church, 'Captain' Boyle's days at sea, and a new intention of asserting manly independence which dies instantly on Juno's unexpected re-entry. She is excited by some sudden news and tells Boyle to take off the moleskin trousers he is wearing in anticipation of going to seek work. Mary enters with Charlie Bentham, another suitor, who gives the news that a week before the death of a Mr Ellison he drew up a will for him, leaving half his property, something between £1,500 and £2,000, to Mr Boyle. Juno's innate snobbery is revealed in the fuss she makes of Bentham. Boyle, elated by the news, offers Bentham a drink and renounces Joxer when he climbs back into the room through the window. Boyle declares that he is a new man, and, singing emotionally, clasps Juno's hand.

The summary above indicates how much O'Casey manages to pack into the first act. The opening description of the scene is a full one, and immediately contributes to the atmosphere of deprivation – two rooms only, a tenement which is one of many. O'Casey's particularity is a reflection of his own familiarity with this life-style, and the details, from the picture of the Virgin to the shovel, each symbolize aspects of the ambience of these working (or non-working) lives. Note the sparse treatment of Johnny in this description – what has happened to him will be revealed in narrative within the text – and the much fuller treatment of Mary, where the impact of environment on her behaviour is fully evident.

The same sense of deprivation is apparent in the first description of Juno, while expectation is aroused by Mary's half-account from the newspaper. We are aware at once of the currency of violence, with Johnny's hysterical reaction understandable in view of what is later revealed. Hints at Boyle's way of life, his irresponsibility, prepare us for the kind of person he is before he enters. Juno is obviously the centre and support of the family, while Johnny's asking for the glass of water to be brought to him shows his insecurity and his need for affection. The speech, given the localized context, is totally convincing: we note O'Casey's use of contrast, Mary being concerned with her appearance (the ribbon), Juno with the practicalities of survival because (it is suggested) of her husband's indolence.

Already the theme of appearance and reality is being sounded, but we register too the realism, the natural interaction of Juno and Mary. This is seen in Mary's determination to appear independent of the employers, and her mother's registering of what she wears as running counter to this. Their conversation reflects the fact that this is a period of change (in employee–employer relationships) as well as one of wider religious and secular conflict.

Johnny's reappearance shows him about to crack with nervous tension, his exit after Juno's account of how he got his injuries leading to another exchange in the battle over 'principle'. Perhaps most poignant at this stage is Johnny's fear of being left alone. His fixation is on the picture of the Virgin and on light, which at the end of the play finally goes out.

Jerry is accurately summed up on his entrance – again he is the product of his place and time – but his motivation here is positive. In these bad times he is obviously thinking how best he can assist the family, and here the news of a job for Boyle underlines Jerry's own feelings. His exit, Juno's recognition of her husband's character and her articulation of it, both these combine to make the first sounds of Boyle and Joxer all the more humorous and (for the waiting Juno) all the more poignant. The description of Boyle almost verges on one-dimensional caricature, but this is a deliberate mode of irony, since his appearance conceals a reality which has already been spelled out for us.

There is the natural comedy of Boyle and Joxer entering, Boyle under the impression that Juno is not there: the audience knows that she is, hence this is an early use of dramatic irony. The focus on Joxer's physical characteristics again reflects how completely O'Casey is with his characters – feeling, seeing, recording – even down to his clichéd utterance 'when the cat's away, the mice can play'. His half-quotation about the cup of tea adds to the humour, since we suspect that he and Boyle are constantly inebriated: the fact that he is 'cut short' borders on farce. This is enhanced by his sudden change of mind when Juno speaks, which is another underlining of the time-wasting and irresponsibility which is the hallmark of the two men.

Boyle now initiates an act with Joxer – the pretence that they might have been in work – knowing that if they are to placate Juno they must convince her of the sincerity of their intentions. Of course the effectiveness of O'Casey's use of irony is seen when Juno prevents them from leaving – she sees how transparent their conversation is ('them yarns won't go down with Juno'). Juno is quickly into full rhetorical stride, lacerating Boyle's hypochondriac tendencies (the constant reference to his legs) and playing brilliantly on the word 'rest'. Her sarcasm is withering and shows the strength of her personality, the quality of the woman. Notice how completely convincing this domestic exchange is – the pace of it is true to life, absolutely vivid with actuality. Boyle cannot wriggle out from under her determination, despite his reflex lying.

At this juncture the entrance of Jerry Devine is dramatic – O'Casey always displays a craftsman's sense of engagement with his audience. The effect here is to thrust Boyle even more on the defensive, so much so that he is forced into going over the top about the pain he (supposedly) feels in his leg. This is direct visual comedy, as Boyle continues to demonstrate his incapacity for work, the physical reasons being the reflex of his conditioned mental state. We note the vividness of Juno's language in response to his affectations, her exit reflecting their way of life, Juno the breadwinner and Boyle the lay-about.

The interaction between Mary and Jerry is underlined by the sharpness of Mary's tongue (you might compare her with her mother) and the sentimental poeticisms of Jerry ('all the happy evenin's that were as sweet as the scented ...'). Again the theme of conflict, mirroring the political and religious conflict, is being sounded. This is extended with the entrance of Boyle, and we feel the oppression of people living on top of one another. The smallness of the apartment means that everything is heard and known. At the back of the argument between Mary and Jerry is the sense of class difference and of social deprivation.

Boyle of course protests too much, particularly about the breakfast. We have noted the excessive sentimentality of Joxer's language and also Jerry's, and now Boyle plunges into sentimental song: it is as if O'Casey is providing a running commentary on the nature of Irish characteristics, which indeed he is. Note that the song carries a certain irony in relation to Mary and Jerry, and that the nature imagery present in it is being used as a counterpoint to the crowded (and unnatural) urban existence lived by the characters in the play.

With Joxer's entrance the natural comedy is somewhat overlaid by the fear of danger, the violence just beneath the surface. Johnny is plainly scared, Boyle and Joxer conspiratorial. Obviously Mary's reading of Ibsen shows how advanced she is for her time (and indeed *A Doll's House* is regarded by many as a major feminist work). The superior 'rank' of the 'Captain' is seen in his apportioning only the gravy to Joxer: he indulges his feelings to Joxer, feeling that Jerry has deliberately put him on the spot by indicating the possibility of work.

He twists and turns in his arguments to avoid any kind of regular employment, his evasions maintaining the comic temperature. But in some of Boyle's assertions there are important comments on the state of Ireland, for example his view that the clergy had too much power. But Boyle is concerned only with himself. Notice the dramatic effect of the coal-vendor's voice coming immediately after Boyle's inveighing against the clergy. His next bout of indulgence is to reinvoke the nature of his (fictitious) past. The comic temperature is again raised by the fear that it is Juno who is coming, the appearance of the coal-vendor providing an effective dramatic anti-climax. Thereafter the exchanges rest on Boyle's bravado and Joxer's encouragement of him: all this is leading up to the real re-entrance of Juno, when Boyle will be put to the test. The audience is therefore being kept on the edge of dramatic expectation. We are not disappointed, Joxer 'flying out of the window' when he hears Juno's voice, having just told the 'Captain' to be firm. Boyle immediately lies (will he be found out again, and always found out?). Notice how the atmosphere of mystery is built up about the coming news.

The entrance of Mary with Charlie Bentham establishes at once the contrast between this young man and Jerry. Juno, in her 'fussing', inadvertently contributes to the humour by saying that Boyle is 'just takin' off his trousers'. The reiteration of this by Johnny with the sound carrying in the confined space adds of course to Mary's embarrassment – and Juno's – and maintains the farcical element of the situation. This is in abeyance when Johnny is introduced by Juno to Bentham, his bravado (about what he has done for Ireland) bearing a certain resemblance to his father's. Juno's observation about arms being the only principles 'that's any good to a workin' man' underlines the social and economic deprivation once again.

Bentham's 'culture' causes him to note the name 'Juno' (and perhaps we ponder its mock-heroic quality here), but the dramatic excitement is generated by the reading of the will, with the fact that the 'first and second cousins' are not named being an important factor. The reactions are predictable – Johnny's exclamation that they can now go where they are not known giving the lie to his previous statement – while the hypocrisy of Boyle is immediately evident in his suggestion that they go into mourning for 'poor Bill', whom he has previously reviled. Joxer's reappearance maintains the comic flow. His parody of Boyle is effective, funny, revealing perhaps more character and personality than we would previously have credited him with. Notice the swiftness with which the change has been effected: money, or the prospect of it, rules the lives of the poor. Joxer's last words are an accurate summary of his (erstwhile) friend's character. Boyle and his recurrence to sentimental song reflect the insecurity of these lives – a minute changes everything, volatility evolves from circumstances.

tenement house Formerly good class town houses in the city which have deteriorated into slum property occupied by a number of families.

Diehard A Republican who was determined to fight against the partition of Ireland into the Irish Free State and Ulster.

boul' Bald.

good Samaritan A person prepared to go out of his way to help others, like the good Samaritan who helped the man who was stripped and beaten by robbers. (Luke 10, 30–7.)

Health Insurance Money paid by the state to a worker whilst he is absent from employment through illness.

dole Money paid by the state to the unemployed.

Novena In the Roman Catholic Church special prayers and services for a particular object or event, performed over nine days.

to walk out To strike.

walk the streets Become a prostitute.

Wan One (dialect).

he's paid He'll never get his money.

Easter Week In Easter 1916, a group of Irishmen seeking independence rose in revolt. The leaders were captured and executed. W. B. Yeats wrote a poem, 'Easter 1916', commemorating it.

O'Connell Street One of the main streets of Dublin which was the scene of fighting during the struggle between the Sinn Feiners and British troops which led to the 'Home Rule' Bill of 1920.

Free State The Irish Free State was set up by the Treaty of 1921, with a Parliament in Dublin and the status of a Dominion of the British Empire.

snug Cosy private bar in a public house.

gets win' o' the'word Hears about it.

affeydavey Affidavit, written statement confirmed on oath.

furrage Forage.

Deirdre of the Sorras A legendary Irish princess and the subject of the last incomplete play by the Irish playwright, J. M. Synge.

the cup that ... A misquotation from *The Task*, Book 4, 'The Winter Evening', by William Cowper (1731–1800): '... the cups/That cheer but not inebriate ...'

butty Friend, crony (dialect).

blow o' dinner The dinner whistle.

moleskins Hard-wearing trousers.

ayse Ease.

navvy A shovel used by a labourer.

Christo For Columbus Christopher Columbus (*c.* 1451–1506), the discoverer of America.

cushy Easy.

hod A builder's trough on a pole for carrying mortar or bricks, over the shoulder.

wake A watching round a corpse to bid farewell.

clicked Fallen in love.

Chiselurs Children.

chassis Chaos. These words are repeated in the final line of the play.

kisser Mouth (slang).

thrench coat A trench coat, worn by soldiers, here probably suggesting a member of the Irish Republican Army.

bog o' Allen Marshy land outside Dublin; it is used here to express contempt for peasants as opposed to Dublin men.

The Doll's House, Ghosts, an' The Wild Duck Plays by the Norwegian dramatist, Henrik Ibsen (1828–1906), dealing with social problems.

Virol A nourishing food made of malt.

Wicklow A mountainous county south of Dublin.

'47 1846 and 1847 were years of famine in Ireland. The peasants in their hunger tried to seize the landlords' wheat. They were too exhausted to present any problem and were quickly put down.

Parnell Charles Stewart Parnell (1846–91) was an Irish politician who hoped to gain Home Rule through his influence in the English Parliament. He fell from power through his alleged adultery with the wife of Captain O'Shea.

The Fenians Irish–American secret society founded in 1858 and pledged to support an Irish Republic.

craw-thumpin' Breast-beating.

Catechism Instruction in the form of question and answer, used by the Church.

marlin-spike A spike made of iron or hard wood used for separating strands of rope.

spunk Courage.

How can ... temples of his gods From 'Horatius' in *Lays of Ancient Rome*, by Lord Macaulay (1800–59):

And how can man die better
Than facing fearful odds,
For the ashes of his fathers,
And the temples of his Gods?

collogin' Gossiping, drinking together (dialect).

Homer Ancient Greek epic poet, author of the *Iliad* and the *Odyssey*. In Roman mythology Juno is the wife of Jupiter and Queen of Heaven.

Sorra many Not many (dialect).

Court of Probate The court where wills are formally 'proved'.

St Vincent de Paul Society St Vincent de Paul (*c.* 1581–1660) was a French Roman Catholic saint. He founded the Lazarists and a sisterhood of charity. The Society exists to help the poor.

wet Drink (dialect).

a jar – a boul A glass of beer.

Requiescat in pace May he rest in peace (Latin).

St Patrick The patron saint of Ireland.

St Bridget Another Irish saint, sometimes known as the Bride of Kildare.

Guh ... ayera *Go Saoraidh Dia Eire*. Gaelic for 'God Save Ireland'.

had a slate off Was mad.

aw rewaeawr Au revoir.

Revision questions on Act 1

1 Describe the relationship between Mr Boyle and Juno as shown in the first Act.

2 What is learnt about the characters of Mary and Johnny in the first Act?

3 Comment on the general quality of the family life revealed in the first Act.

4 Choose two incidents that arouse humour. Describe them briefly and assess the kind and quality of humour.

Act 2

Notice the immediate register of change in the over-crowding of the 'vulgar' furniture and knick-knacks, the flowers are artificial (like this 'change' in their lives), all undertaken in a very short passage of time. Song heralds Joxer's entrance, flamboyance marks Boyle's description of his 'work' arising from his new-found wealth. Boyle, characteristically, has already borrowed on the strength of his great expectations (there is some pathos here): both he and Joxer are living the romance of this new situation, with Joxer even invoking romantic literature (inaccurately) through his reference to 'the two Musketeers'. At the same time Joxer is able to bring his own irony to bear on the situation. Boyle has turned about face in his attitude towards the clergy: again this shows how insecure he is, with the new respectability driving him on, so much so, that in his reference to the Fenians and Parnell he contradicts what he said in the first act.

Boyle's comments on Mary's two suitors are interesting: he recognizes that they are opposites (or are they, under their skins?), and we feel that he resents each of them because they challenge his own sense of self-importance. That importance is reinforced by the purchase of the gramophone – it puts him one up in his small world – and we note that, characteristically, it is Juno who does the carrying, and the worrying. The focus of her worry is Johnny, his insecurity and fear of reprisals causing him to sleep in different places, obviously in the hope that he won't be traced. Again we remember his bravado about what he has done for Ireland, and we are going to be reminded even more forcibly before the end of the act. His repetition of words and phrases – a kind of neurotic stutter – shows the abject state he is in. Boyle's sarcasm at the expense of Bentham stresses his resentment of the man (and perhaps some possessiveness over Mary). At the same time there is a class resentment too: he tries to show himself superior by the mention of 'Consols', and there is comedy in the fact that he really has no idea of what he is talking about.

There follows a cameo – the interaction between Mary and Bentham set against Boyle's determination to be centre stage and to make portentous statements as well as commanding from his new position of authority – even if he only gets 'Tay'. Juno rises to the occasion too by imitating what she feels is intelligent comment on the state of the Irish world. But Bentham undermines this social simulation by telling them that he is a Theosophist. O'Cassey's irony is here combined with Boyle's own ironic appraisal of what he is being told (and his misunderstanding of some of it). But a dangerous note has entered the action with the mention of ghosts and death, particularly the idea of a place being associated with what happened there. It precipitates hysteria from Johnny, who literally has been unable to escape from his experiences. We sense in his 'confession' to his mother a very strong sense of guilt, that he may have been responsible for the death of Robin Tancred. The area of superstition in the human mind is seen in the fact that finally Bentham himself has to go into the room to see if the light is burning before the statue.

The description of Mrs Madigan – a type strongly individualized by the density of O'Casey's description – has strong overtones of pathos, but perhaps more of fear that she would be capable of injuring what she was trying to save. The extravagant praise heaped on her by Boyle and Joxer is grotesque: her own language, full of extravagance and simulated nostalgia, exactly suits her description. Boyle's effusiveness cannot still Juno's sharp tongue (note here the wonderful interpretation of 'tight corner'), and nothing is going to prevent Mrs Madigan from having a drink, or from reminiscing: the comedy of her reminiscing – perhaps romancing would be a better word – almost makes her a stereotypical Irish character from farce. The sentimental song – and Boyle's indulgently sentimental response to it – shows the edge of O'Cassey's irony – while Mrs Madigan once more takes over the conversation (though hardly the singing). Joxer's inadequacy is shown in his failure to finish his songs, but we feel that the party – for that's what it is at this stage – is a selfish indulgence beside the serious happenings close by. Juno sounds the sober note with her news of Mrs Tancred: the latter typifies the tragedy of Ireland, and there is a fine and sharp play on words here ('king-pauper'). Mrs Tancred's grief, as wordy as Mrs Madigan's reminiscences, does not strike us as self-indulgent, but rather as the expression of bewilderment at the failure of religion to prevail to save her son.

Again O'Casey is working his dramatic effects through a fine sense of contrast. With the exit of Mrs Tancred and the mourning group we have a further insight into Johnny's hysteria, seen in his reaction to his mother's explanatory remarks to Bentham about the dead man. Bentham himself shows how reactionary he is in his 'mad dog' reference, but notice that Boyle distances himself – as so many would wish to – from the events. Juno's impassioned response is the measure of her commitment to life – and here, in the middle of life, they are in death. Her rhetoric indicates the widespread nature of the violence and its effects – ironically, the full measure of these effects is to be brought out later. Boyle reacts as we have come to expect that he would – by recurring to his (fantasy) past and affecting to be cynical. Joxer's casual rhyming couplet is also a comment on the events by which these people are surrounded. Juno continues with her invective, but it is important to note that she too fixes some of the blame for what has happened on Mrs Tancred because of her 'open house' attitude towards the Die-hards. At this stage she seems oblivious of the effect on Johnny, who still continues to fear all this talk.

The transition to song reflects the volatility of the group – a volatility deriving either from the Irish temperament, their situation, or perhaps just the need to escape from that situation in this way. One moment life is intensely serious, the next song provides the relief. Boyle, conscious of his new status through the inheritance, comes centre stage with his song. The words are sentimental but have some ironic currency in the present situation. Seemingly forgetful of Mrs Tancred's grief, the whole group suggest that the gramophone is played. This precipitates the dramatic arrival of Nugent: we feel that in fact there is no escape from the tragic situation in which they are all caught up. Juno reacts strongly – and superficially – as does Mrs Madigan, but they are overtaken by the noise in the street, the singing, the coming of the hearse. In a sense, this emotional moment has replaced the simulated emotionalism of the indoor singing. The principle of contrast continues to operate. With the exit of everyone except Johnny, the entrance of the young man is a dramatic stroke – the one-to-one situation, filled with menace, with threat – which fills the audience with expectation of events to come. Note the religious singing, an ironic counterpart to the action, for certainly religious differences, which account in major part for the violence, have bred in people an extremist fervour which can resolve nothing. And the young man's final remark is expressive of a fanaticism which is paradoxically un-Christian in its creed.

A few days have passed since the end of the first Act. The scene is the same room but there is more furniture, all tasteless. Ornaments and artificial flowers fill every space. Boyle is stretched out half asleep on the sofa. When he hears Joxer he busies himself with papers to give an air of self-importance.

Boyle and Joxer are clearly friends again. Boyle, feeling more secure in his new-found wealth, is less afraid of his wife and jovially invites Joxer in. Boyle's opinion of the Church has significantly changed, he forbids Joxer to condemn Father Farrell. Boyle is hostile to the developing relationship between Bentham and Mary, founded on his dislike of the young man's superior manner and knowledge. Juno enters, with Mary, carrying a gramophone. Johnny is in a disturbed restless state, sleeping one night at his Aunt's and one night at home. He asserts he can rest nowhere. Bentham enters, heralded by Boyle's objecting to the fuss Juno makes of him. Boyle repeats his pessimistic view of the state of the country. Bentham expounds his Theosophy. When they talk of ghosts Johnny becomes very agitated. He goes into the other room but soon rushes out again in an hysterical state. He claims to have seen the ghost of the dead Robbie Tancred kneeling before the statue of the Virgin. Bentham goes in after Boyle has asked Mary to go.

Bentham finds nothing amiss. Mrs Madigan, a middle-aged neighbour, enters. They all settle down to drink, to reminisce, and to sing. As Boyle prepares to start the gramophone they hear Mrs Tancred and a number of neighbours passing on their way to the hospital where her son's body lies. Mary opens the door and Mrs Boyle invites Mrs Tancred in for a cup of tea. She refuses, and launches into an expression of sorrow for her own poverty and the loss of her son. Boyle claims to have no interest in the deaths of those who have dedicated themselves to the cause of Irish Nationalism; Juno is deeply concerned. However, they return to their drinking and to playing the gramophone. 'Needle' Nugent, the tailor, protests. They abuse him. The sound of a crowd singing heralds the appearance of the hearse. They all go down to the street for a better view. Johnny is left alone. A young man enters to order him to attend a Battalion Staff meeting. He refuses to go, protesting that he has done enough for Ireland. The young man replies that no man can do enough for Ireland,

and the words of the Ave Maria are heard from the crowd in the distance.

attackey Attaché.

the two Musketeers An incorrect reference to *The Three Musketeers*, by Alexandre Dumas (1802–70), with its motto: 'All for one and one for all'.

I met with Napper Tandy From the famous song, *The Wearing of the Green*, adopted by the Irish revolutionaries. It was written in 1798 and known in Irish as 'Shan Van Voght'. James Napper Tandy (1740–1803) was the first Secretary of the Society of United Irishmen.

heart o' the rowl Excellent man.

bummer Idler.

Soggart Aroon Dear priest (Gaelic).

J. L. Sullivan Boyle is mocking Joxer. J. L. Sullivan (usually referred to as John L. Sullivan) was a heavyweight boxing champion.

Boney's Oraculum A collection of predictions. Napoleon Bonaparte was often referred to as Boney; he was reputed to have believed in the power of astrology.

wrong shipped Deluded.

allanna My love (Gaelic).

Consols Government securities of Great Britain consolidated into a single stock in 1751.

when we got the makin' of our own laws Under the Treaty of 1921.

Theosophist Theosophy, a system of religious belief derived mainly from eastern mysticism, was founded by Madame Blavatsky in 1875; she also formed the Theosophical Society to propagate the doctrine, which is essentially that knowledge of God is sought through meditation or direct communion.

The Vedas The four sacred books of the Indian Brahmins. *Veda* means 'knowledge' in Sanskrit.

Prawna Breath (Sanskrit).

Yogi Those who practise Yoga, a system of physical postures designed to concentrate the mind and to attain union (the Sanskrit meaning of Yoga). In spite of the cosmopolitan nature of San Francisco, it is highly unlikely that Boyle has seen hundreds of Yogi in its streets.

Tommy Mix Tom Mix, a cowboy, was one of the heroes of silent Western films.

I seen him This is Robbie Tancred, whose death reported in the morning paper is referred to by Mary at the opening of the play. Johnny's hysteria is only too well justified by future events.

right as the mail Fully recovered.

shuk Shaken, possibly injured.

bit o' skirt A vulgar term for a girl that expresses Mrs Madigan's character.

skelpin' Slap.

commensurate A malapropism, showing that her delight in using long words is not backed by her knowledge of them.

Shamrock A plant, the symbol of Ireland. Here Boyle is mocking both his friend and the Irish movement.

Nil desperandum Never despair (Latin).

suspicious Another malapropism.

Gawn Go on. Cf. the cockney 'Garn', as used by Eliza in Shaw's *Pygmalion*.

doty Decayed.

green, white an' orange The Irish colours.

the Tans A force specially formed for the Irish War, consisting of English soldiers who had fought in the Great War, though not part of the British Army. They wore no particular uniform at first, but their dress included Army khaki and black leather belts.

Jazz dancin' A cynical description of the ruthlessness of the British troops which horrified world opinion.

natural Life.

She is far from the lan' A song by Thomas Moore (1779–1852), an Irish poet.

I have heard the mavis From the popular song, *Mary of Argyle*, by Charles Jefferys (1807–65). The mavis is a thrush.

Republicans Those who were hostile to the Dominion status conferred by the Treaty of 1921 and wanted an independent Irish republic.

Free State soldier son The Irish Free State Army fought against the Republicans.

made a collandher of i.e. full of holes.

C.I.D. Criminal Investigation Department, a branch of the police force.

Civic Guards The police set up by the Irish Free State.

Pillar Nelson's Pillar in O'Connell Street. The column was blown up in 1966.

gave the bend Informed.

Hail, Mary... From the Angel Gabriel's words to the Virgin Mary. The words are an ironic commentary on the death of sons and the sorrows of mothers – one of the themes of this Act.

Revision questions on Act 2

1 Show how the expectation of money effects a change in the relationship between Boyle and Juno.

2 What impact does the hope of wealth have upon the lives of the Boyle family?

3 What is the dramatic purpose of the drinking and singing episode?

4 Johnny is a constant reminder of the political scene. Describe how this is shown in the second Act.

Act 3

Two months have passed since the end of the last Act. It is a November evening. Mary sits dejectedly. Mrs Boyle questions her about Bentham, whom Mary has neither seen nor heard from for a month. Mary declares her love for him. Juno is worried about Mary's health and is taking her to the doctor that evening. Boyle, in the next room, complains about the pain in his legs. He has, as yet, received none of the money he was left in the Will. They are deeply in debt. Juno and Mary leave for the doctor's. Soon Joxer enters with Nugent, the tailor. They, believing there is no one at home, discuss Boyle's debts; when Boyle coughs they realize the flat is not empty. Nugent leaves, taking with him the suit that Boyle has not yet paid for, and is suspected of stealing the bottle of stout that Joxer has slipped into his pocket. Mrs Madigan enters and removes the gramophone to pawn it against the money that Boyle owes her. Boyle and Joxer quarrel about whether Boyle is ever going to get the money left to him. Joxer leaves as Johnny enters, followed shortly by a thoughtful Juno.

Boyle is angry and shattered when he learns that Mary is pregnant, and shows no sympathy for her predicament. Juno is determined to shelter and support her and to leave with her if Boyle still refuses to help. Johnny takes his father's side. Boyle, in his fury, tells Juno that there will be no money from the Will: Bentham had bungled it by not mentioning Boyle by name. Juno realizes now why Bentham has deserted Mary. Johnny, angry at the debts Boyle has accumulated, turns on his father. Juno tries to pacify him. Boyle goes out with Joxer for a drink. Johnny blames his mother for giving way to his father. At this point two men come in to collect the furniture, which has not been paid for. Johnny pleads with his mother to fetch his father. Mary enters and Juno blurts out how everything has gone wrong, and goes off to find Boyle. Jerry Devine enters. He offers Mary his love and support – until he discovers she is pregnant. He leaves, and Mary, overwhelmed by Johnny's mean dishonesty, rushes out. Johnny reveals his hysterical fear to the men removing the furniture. Two Irregulars enter, tell the furniture removers to stand with their faces to the wall, and take Johnny with them, first reminding him of his treachery which was responsible for Tancred's death.

An hour later Mary and Juno have returned to sit in a darkened room with little furniture left in it. Juno is worried about her son. Mrs Madigan comes to tell her that two policemen are below asking her to go to the hospital to see Johnny's body. She determines to go without Mary, whom she sends to her sister's. She bitterly condemns her own lack of sympathy for Mrs Tancred when her son was found shot, and prays to the Virgin Mary that love should take the place of murderous hate. Boyle enters with Joxer when the women have left; both drunkenly express their spurious patriotism. Finally, Boyle repeats his contention that the world is in a terrible state of chaos.

Once more the stage directions are important. The ending of Act II with its blessing of the Virgin Mary finds this Mary now unvirginal and depressed (note the effect of the light glowing under the picture). The desertion of Bentham has obviously precipitated this crisis, though we are soon to be aware that his deceptions have far-reaching effects. There is a terrible irony in Juno asserting that Bentham 'couln't have been thinkin' of the money' when in fact he is responsible, as we are shortly to discover, for there not being any. In the conversation between Juno and Mary we note the emphasis on the class divisions in this society, as well as the generation gap between mother and daughter which makes genuine communication between them so difficult.

The atmosphere generated by O'Casey in this third act is an oppressive one: Boyle's 'pains in me legs' is no longer funny but symptomatic of the fear that everything has gone wrong, while Juno's mention of the asylum and the Poorhouse is too close for comfort.

Nugent's own investigations, dominated as they are by self-interest, merely prove what we have suspected, namely that Boyle has been 'conned' into believing that there is money coming to him. The dramatic effect here is achieved through the dramatic irony of the audience knowing that Boyle can hear every derogatory word that is being said about him, with Joxer taking the lead in putting him down.

The taking of the suit marks the end of Boyle's pretensions, but Joxer's interaction with Boyle takes on an unpleasant tinge, underlining his shallowness of nature. We remember that he has taken the stout, the only comfort within Boyle's reach, but his affectation that it is Nugent who is to be despised for this shows his capacity to turn on the lies: what was laughable earlier in the play is now evidence of hypocrisy. His flippancy in doggerel when Mrs Madigan enters shows that he is enjoying the humiliation of the impoverished Boyle. Mrs Madigan herself complements Joxer by her own role and her insistence on payment: we can't help looking back to the convivial gathering in which she and Joxer took part, and contrasting the attitudes then and now. The peacock image used by her as she seizes the gramophone is now doubly ironic: Boyle, to continue the figurative language, has hardly any feathers left. Joxer now delights in the home truths he can tell Boyle, going as usual into doggerel as he does so. We note now that there is no let-up in the action; Johnny's entrance is followed by that of his mother without Mary, with the dramatic temperature again rising. Her revelation – bearing in mind the time at which the play is set – is almost the final blow at their respectability. Typically, Boyle receives the news with the self-pity that we have come to associate with him. Juno's character, her sense of perspective, is admirable, and contrasts at every turn with that of her husband. In the quarrel which follows the expected accusations come out, with Boyle ascribing Mary's moral fall to her reading. O'Casey is here uttering profound truths about people – how they feel that they will be talked about and disgraced, their images of themselves permanently dented. The male attitude – reinforced by Johnny's quick-to-blame voice – is here contrasted with the women's attitude of compassion and understanding. With Boyle's revelation that there is no money coming to them we might say that the exterior 'troubles' of Ireland are being carefully mirrored by this interior suffering, and of course the two are to be brought together with the killing of Johnny. The tragedy is unremitting from now onwards. O'Casey, in exposing the nature of Bentham's error, is also exposing human nature and its inherent greed, something we have seen throughout the play, and more particularly in this act. Of course legal loopholes are also being displayed.

All this is too much for Johnny – note the pace of this act, where something is happening all the time in terms of action. For the characters and the audience there is no respite. There is part of us which, we suspect, feels that Boyle deserves what he gets: but we must weigh this against the social conditions of the time for Boyle and his kind, conditions which they did not make but which have effectively reduced them. When Johnny denounces his father the ultimate in family conflict has been achieved. Boyle returns to his own vomit – Joxer – like a dog. He has no reserves with which to face his degradation.

Johnny's action in throwing himself on the bed has its own part in the structure of the play: his wish for a past death is soon to be realized in the immediate present. Before that he manages to blame his mother for indulging his father, and we are aware, as in most arguments, that there is some truth in his assertion, though our sympathies are certainly with Juno when she says that she has been responsible for keeping the family together. Mary's entrance, Johnny's criticism of her, then Jerry's entrance, all these emphasize the speed of the action. The fact that Jerry has *not* been told that Mary is pregnant ensures that what I have called the unremitting nature of the tragedy is maintained. Mary, who has said little, has the clinching line of the scene when she observes 'your humanity is just as narrow as the humanity of the others'. The song is a poignant and superb comment on the nature of human nature, the hell that man has made for himself on earth. It is immediately evidenced by the men coming for Johnny and taking him away to execute him. The conflict is epitomized by Mary's rejection of God and her mother's defence 'Ah, what can God do agen the stupidity o' men?' Juno's great speech in which she blames herself for not thinking enough of Mrs Tancred's suffering shows her capacity for deep feeling. She echoes Mrs Tancred's own words, but her prayer to Jesus is an impassioned one. Notice Joxer's First World War song, which echoes the permanent war in which the Irish find themselves. Drunkenness here reflects the chaos of man caught in the chaos of strife, religious, social and political, which wrecks living. The troubles which bring chaos, and which continue, and continue, and continue, underline the terrible realism at the end of the play.

Sloan's Liniment An old-established remedy for muscular pain and stiffness.

red rex A penny, rex meaning king (Latin) because it bears the king's head.

make A halfpenny.

an honest man's From *Easy on Man* by Alexander Pope (1688–1744).

redshank Kind of snipe, a gamebird with red legs.

man's inhumanity From *Man was made to Mourn*, by Robert Burns (1759–96).

barny Little talk.

formularies A malapropism for 'formalities'.

uncle's Pawnbroker's.

sup taken Been drinking.

gradle Lot.

St Anthony St Anthony (251–356) was the first advocate of the monastic ideal.

The Little Flower St Theresa of Lisieux (1873–97). She advocated the Little Way of Goodness in small things in daily life and is known as Little Flower of Jesus.

Child o' Mary A Roman Catholic society for the young is called the Children of Mary.

thick Idiot.

banjax Mess.

world an' his wife Everybody, a vast number of men and women.

whisht Be quiet.

beads Rosary. He will need to say his prayers before he dies.

Null an' Void A legal expression meaning amounting to nothing.

The last o' the Mohicans *The Last of the Mohicans*, a novel by James Fenimore Cooper (1789–1851), in which appears Uncas, an Indian chief.

Put all ... your throubles From a popular song of the First World War, *Pack Up Your Troubles in Your Old Kit-Bag*.

Breathes there a man with soul From *The Lay of the Last Minstrel*, by Sir Walter Scott (1771–1832): 'Breathes there the man, with soul so dead ...'

Willy ... Reilly ... Colleen ... Bawn A ballad that tells the story of a rich girl's love for a nationalist.

Revision questions on Act 3

1 'The balance is tipped in the third Act from comedy to horror.' Discuss.

2 'Juno has the stuff of the tragic heroine.' How far do the events in the final Act and her reactions to them substantiate this statement?

3 'Whatever sympathy the audience may have had for Boyle is lost in this Act.' How far do you agree with this?

4 What hope in life is still left at the end of the final Act?

The characters

'Captain' Jack Boyle

... an' he shruttin' about from mornin' till night like a paycock!

When the play opens Boyle is away from home drinking; at the end he enters the tenement room, very drunk. Drinking is his main occupation – Boyle drinks as other men work.

He is about sixty years old, stout, grey-haired and stocky. His head, with his short neck, is likened to a stone ball on top of a gate-post. There is a clipped moustache on his upper lip, and his cheeks are the reddish-purple of the heavy drinker. To bolster the 'captain' image he wears a peaked seaman's cap. He struts with his body leaning backwards and his stomach thrown forward; his slow, self-important walk gives rise to the 'Paycock' of the title.

At the start of the play Boyle is afraid of his wife, and complains that she is always grumbling; and grumble she does, when she appears. He will lie, swear, plead excuses and wallow in self-pity in his attempts to appease her – to no avail, for his lies and excuses are glaringly obvious to her. Yet he is not downtrodden. When he is promised a legacy in the Will, some of the mastery of which he doubtless boasts in the snug in Ryan's or Foley's is evident.

His lies, like those of Falstaff, are gross, so that the audience wonders whether they are meant only to deceive or whether in his hands they are a form of art, conceived in the imagination and lovingly embroidered. Of such perhaps is the story of the job which he is to seek. The pain in his legs that manifests itself whenever work is mentioned is a recurring theme that becomes inextricably bound up with his character.

He is a thoroughly idle waster, yet socially he has an abundance of vitality. He can keep a party going with drink, wit and song. He is determined that not even Mrs Tancred's passing to collect the body of her murdered son shall interrupt his merrymaking: 'We've nothin' to do with these things, one way or t'other.'

He has no right to the title of Captain, except in his own imagination: 'Them was days, Joxer, them was days ... Sailin' from the Gulf o' Mexico to the Antanartic Ocean. I seen things, I seen things, Joxer, that no mortal man should speak about' (p.23); in reality, he was 'only wanst on the wather, in an oul' collier from here to Liverpool' (p.14).

Boyle is a bad parent and a faithless friend; when he thinks he has come into money he is willing to finish with Joxer, though, in fairness to him, he does not do so. He has neither realization nor care for Johnny's suffering, and when Mary ignores him when she is with Jerry her contempt for him is obvious.

'Chiselurs don't care a damn now about their parents,' he complains. When he learns that Mary is pregnant he can think only of raging and driving her out of the house, and he is not to be moved from this course even by the threat of Juno's leaving. He has the self-sufficiency of the thoroughly egotistical and selfish: 'I lived before I seen yous, an' I can live when yous are gone' (p.62). He is completely insensitive to other people's feelings, and can mock and insult his friend Joxer to his face. When he finally tells Juno about the money he is totally blunt and direct – there is no attempt to break the news gently to her.

He is a snob. '... you're to keep yourselves to yourselves for the future' (p.30) he tells Johnny and Mary after hearing the news of the Will. Plainly, however, he is too sociable to carry out his snobbery, and is more than prepared to welcome the Mrs Madigans of the world into his home.

The furnishing of the room, in anticipation of his new-found wealth, reveals his innate lack of taste. His pomposity shows in his pretence of busying himself with documents to impress Joxer, and speaking self-importantly of the responsibility of money. Yet in some ways he is more independent than his wife. He does not fuss around Bentham as she does, but he cannot resist the temptation to show off by talking about Consols and the state of the country.

His cowardice is manifest; he is quite prepared to send Mary into the other room rather than go himself when he thinks Johnny might have seen a ghost. His talk is big, his action despicable.

His politics, like everything else in his life, are based on self-interest. He is a great man for leaving things to the government, a confirmed non-participator and non-thinker, one who denies all responsibility but nevertheless a great grumbler, chiefly expressed in the oft-repeated statement that the whole world is 'in a terrible state o' chassis'.

Despite all this, Boyle is a rich source of humour, and for that alone the audience will love him and forgive him much. We enjoy his naming of Juno 'Deirdre of the Sorras', his regret that there is no brass band to play Bentham in, or the idea that the sea is always calling him. Occasionally his wit is based on shrewdness and self-knowledge. 'It's a curious way to reward Johnny be makin' his poor oul' father work' (p.22) he asserts wryly.

A fine sense of language informs all his speech; he can work up to a powerful peroration, and is not inhibited by too close a concern with the exact meaning of a long word: 'Well, let him give his job to wan of his hymn-singin', prayer-spoutin', craw-thumpin' Confraternity men!' (p.22).

Boyle also has a nice sense of rhythm, and his reiteration is a delight to the ear. Sometimes his humour is unintentional but benefits from the dogmatism of his ignorance, as his dismissal of Ibsen's three problem plays as three stories – 'buks only fit for chiselurs!'

He is no figure of tragedy; secure in his armour of survival his losses at the end will hardly touch him. The truth is not in him. As his pregnant daughter has already become 'that lovely daughter o' mine', so will he order all the other events to fit the pattern that makes for a fine tale to tell in the snugs.

He is indeed 'Jacky Boyle Esquire, infernal rogue and damned liar!'

Juno Boyle

'An' who'll have to bear th' biggest part o' this throuble but me?'

Juno plays the tragic heroine to her husband's clown. Sean O'Casey liked to create such mother figures, perhaps inspired by the memory of his own mother, who had brought him up lovingly and carefully amidst the most dire poverty.

Yet Juno is no saint; she is a real woman with real faults. Even a saint would become impatient with the lies and boastings of her husband – decidedly Juno does. She shows a certain ruthlessness in making it clear to him that she is not deceived by him; perhaps this is all part of the game of their relationship – he cannot really imagine that she is taken in by his stories of jobs and the sea. But she can be deceived in circumstance, if not in character, and Boyle succeeds in keeping the truth about the Will from her for some little time.

Juno is fifteen years younger than her husband. Her youthful prettiness has gone, leaving in its place the careworn features characteristic of the overworked, permanently worried women of her class and time in Ireland. She has sufficient personality to force her unruly husband to be circumspect with her and is generally firm in her dealings with him. She grumbles about his cheerfulness, and objects to his singing when he ought, in her view, to be on his knees praying for a job. Johnny's condemnation of Juno for allowing Boyle to have his own way in everything springs out of a particular set of circumstances. Certainly we should not expect her remonstrations with her husband to be anything but honest and straightforward. Vindictiveness and a deliberately planned campaign to bring him to submission would be alien to her nature – in any case, it would not succeed.

She works for, cares for, and organizes her family who, in

return, have little realization of the burdens she carries. From Boyle we would expect no sympathy, but even Mary shows little compassion for her difficulties in shopping without money. Johnny is too immersed in his own problems to do anything other than demand support from his mother, and if she *is* always grousing she has very good cause.

Juno is a respecter of persons; when Bentham visits them she fusses around him, hoping to make a good impression – one that she unwittingly destroys by referring to her husband's removal of his trousers. She is a realist; she has to be.

There is an element of comedy in the choice of her name. She was born and christened in June, married in June, gave birth to a son in June – so Boyle called her Juno.

She has a ready yet practical sympathy; her concern for Mrs Tancred is expressed by inviting her in for a cup of tea. She is politically conscious and disapproves of her husband's philosophy of leaving all to the government. Disappointed that independence has not brought the promised benefits, she wisely remarks that there is too little foresight and care for the future.

Her views mirror very clearly those of O'Casey himself, and his closest identification with any character in the play is with Juno. She, like himself, has very little time for the forms of religion, believing that if people followed up their beliefs more wholeheartedly the world would be a better place.

When disaster strikes the family Juno grows in stature. Her attitude to Mary is a lesson in tolerance and understanding – she will go to any lengths to support her daughter. She does not hesitate to leave her husband to be with Mary in her trouble. Although she thinks that if anything happened to Johnny she would be broken, in the event she rises to the desperate truth of his death with magnificent assurance. After a momentary and understandable indulgence in her own grief, she thinks only of Mary; she knows she has the strength to face the situation alone.

Juno hardly fits the conventional Greek pattern for the tragic heroine; she bears little responsibility for the events that overtake her, either in terms of character or action. She hardly begins the play in a state of flourishing prosperity, though no doubt her end is worse than her beginning. She is the archetypal mother, yet in spite of her maternal concern and care her family disintegrates before her eyes and she is powerless to prevent it. Her nobility is revealed not in the substance of her life within the family but in her manner of reacting to its destruction and in the widening and deepening of her sensibility and understanding.

Johnny Boyle

'Good God, haven't I done enough for Ireland?'

It is difficult to portray effectively on the stage a character living in a constant state of fear bordering on hysteria. Plainly there is a specific reason for his condition, but this is not made clear until the play progresses. The irony implicit in Mrs Boyle's thanking God that Johnny had nothing to do with Mrs Tancred's son cannot be appreciated by the audience at this stage.

In this play, where the political background is important, it is strange that the one character who is actively involved with the nationalists remains throughout a shadowy figure. He obviously feels that his past sacrifices justify the demands he makes on his family, though his ever-present state of fright may, to some extent, excuse him. Mary is right, however, when she points out to her mother that Johnny is big and able enough to get his own drink of water. He is terrified of being left on his own, and objects to the noise made by the neighbours. He is younger than Mary, and slim, pale and delicate; he lost an arm and injured a hip in the rising of Easter 1916, living on the glory of it ever since: 'I'd do it agen ... a principle's a principle' – a boast contrasting oddly with his fear. When we learn more of his circumstances, we realize that he is both a coward and a traitor.

Johnny's own suffering does nothing to increase his compassion towards others; he is harsh and censorious to Mary in her trouble, and despicably dishonest in his advice to her on the way she should have dealt with Jerry. He even upbraids Juno when he discovers the extent of their debts.

The nature of his character is not so much a direct criticism of the nationalist movement itself as a comment on the weak and cowardly men who are sometimes attracted to such movements and who later capitalize on their sacrifices. In his death we feel little sorrow for him but much for Juno.

Mary Boyle

'I couldn't help loving him.'

Mary is a pretty girl of twenty-two, with a good figure. Although she has been brought up in a slum tenement she is trying, as did O'Casey himself, to educate herself by reading. Her choice of Ibsen's plays indicates that she is a girl of some potential intelligence, yet her reaction to her mother's attack on the strike ('a principle's a principle') indicates intellectual limitations. She has scant sympathy with her mother's trials, is distinctly hostile to her brother, and has little, if any, respect for her father. Her vanity is revealed in her preoccupation with the choice of colour for the ribbon she will wear round her head.

Her rejection of Jerry is decisive, perhaps cruel, but then no girl would be at her best in such circumstances. Plainly her socialist principles are insufficient to form an abiding link between them. Her motives here are not quite clear: perhaps, initially, she sees Bentham as the better proposition socially, but later she acknowledges that Jerry is the better man. Or perhaps, as Boyle says, it is her aspirations which have confused her: 'What did th' likes of her, born in a tenement house, want with readin'? Her readin's afther bringin' her to a nice pass' (p.61). Yet she has far less self-pity – and a good deal more pride – than Johnny, for she can keep her misfortunes to herself. Towards the end she gains in nobility; she is open and honest with Jerry, and blames the human condition generally rather than Jerry in particular when he deserts her. When she hears of Johnny's death, she is intelligent in her disillusionment; hers is a powerful cry of revolt.

'Joxer' Daly

'I always knew you were a prognosticator an' a procrastinator!'

Joxer Daly is a caricature, but a very funny one. He is the perfect foil to Boyle who, without him, would be far less amusing. His favourite catchword is 'darlin'' and it is surprising how often and how variously he can use it. Although he will switch his opinion at a moment's notice to suit Boyle's mood or thought, he has no delusions about his friend's character – when he is roused he is very outspoken: 'Sure, you can't believe a word that comes out o' your mouth!'

His fear of Juno leads to a number of comic incidents in the first Act, at the end of which she fails utterly to appreciate his irony and shows him the door, telling him that she 'was always thinkin' you had a slate off'.

He will never express himself in his own words when quotations will do; they range from Pope to Sir Walter Scott, and, drunk or sober, Joxer can always come up with something appropriate.

He has no real part in the plot but is one of the two people on the stage at the end of the play, very drunk, still singing popular songs, still quoting and doubtless still grinning with his crinkled face, cunning twinkle in his eyes.

Jerry Devine

'. . . your humanity is just as narrow as the humanity of the others.'

Jerry belongs to the trade union movement in which O'Casey himself had once played a part. He is about twenty-five, serious, well-built and energetic. He is cool and reasonable: he explains calmly why he is seeking Boyle, ignoring the ill-tempered outburst that results from Boyle's outright lie to Juno being found out.

Jerry would make a good husband for Mary; he loves her, and is confident of his future in the union – he is certain that his popularity and ability in speaking will secure him the Secretaryship.

He is a persistent young man, not easily deterred by Mary's attitude towards him. His recollection of their walk in the country shows an observant eye for nature and a lively capacity for sentiment. The fact that he is capable of influencing Mary is reflected in her reaction to the strike.

Yet, in the end, he is found wanting. When he thinks Mary and Bentham have finished with each other he pleads his cause eloquently, interlacing his political convictions with his expression of love: 'With Labour, Mary, humanity is above everything; we are the Leaders in the fight for a new life ... I want to forget that you left me – even for a while' (p.66). His attitude undergoes a swift change when he learns that Mary is pregnant, and he beats a hasty retreat. This is human and understandable, but it does call into question the sincerity both of his words and his socialist ideals.

Charles Bentham

'The scoundrel, I might ha' known what he was, with his
yogees an' his prawna!'

Bentham plays an utterly ignoble character in the play; he is the dressed-up, 'thin, lanky strip of a Micky Dazzler' who has supplanted Jerry in Mary's affections. A former school-teacher, he is now training to be a solicitor. He is superior and a prig; his culture is unctuous when he speaks of 'Homer's glorious story'. His exposition of his religious thought is grotesque in this particular setting (p.36) and he is not halted by his listeners' comments. He has more courage, or less belief in the supernatural, than Boyle, for he is not afraid to find out whether Johnny's terror is justified. He is somewhat incompetent, however – witness his drawing up of the Will. Juno assumes that he has left Mary because he knew there was no money coming, although it is not made clear whether his courtship began before or after he knew about the Will. He is no credit to humanity, and justifies Juno's question whether there is 'not even a middlin' honest man left in the world'. Yet Mary loved him, even though she realized that he was a lesser man than Jerry – this alone makes his flight to England without leaving an address even more despicable. Mary gives as her reason for his leaving the fact that they 'weren't ... good enough for him', but whether or not he knew she was pregnant is not made clear.

Mrs Maisie Madigan

'... if she could help it at all, ud never see a body shuk!'

Mrs Madigan is a comic character in the tradition of Chaucer's Wife of Bath, Shakespeare's Mistress Quickly and Synge's Widow Quin. She is about forty-five, small but strong, birdlike in manner. She is vulgar, loquacious and self-satisfied; her language and her ideas swing from the crude to the sentimental. Mary she describes to the superior Bentham as a 'nice bit o' skirt'. She has a mind for the dull, trivial details of events that happened long ago, whether it be Mary's birth or her own courting days. When she speaks it is at great length.

She is good-hearted, as she demonstrates by rushing out to fetch a shawl for Mrs Tancred when Juno refers to the coldness of the night. She reveals the closeness of the community that exists in the tenement and the way the lives of its inhabitants have long been bound together. She is capable of violence – she shakes Boyle furiously when she demands the return of her money; when this is not forthcoming she walks off with the gramophone, symbol of Boyle's hopes of prosperity, declaring: 'You're not goin' to be swankin' it like a paycock with Maisie Madigan's money – I'll pull some o' th' gorgeous feathers out o' your tail!' (p.59). Maisie is a better woman to drink and be merry with than to cross.

Themes

A quality shared by the three great Irish dramatists – Oscar Wilde, Bernard Shaw and Sean O'Casey – is that they place very little emphasis on the formal development of a plot. In *Juno and the Paycock* there is a good deal of talk of violence, but very little representation of it. Like Synge in *The Playboy of the Western World*, O'Casey observes a complete unity of place; everything happens in one room. The nearest approach to violent action is in the visits paid to Johnny by the two Irregulars. Yet there is constant movement – exits and entrances, Joxer climbing in through the window and bounding into the room, furniture being moved, Johnny rushing back into the room believing he has seen the dead Robbie Tancred.

The essential drama lies in the talk and the interaction of the characters; in Shaw it is the ideas, in Wilde it is the wit, in O'Casey it is the characterization and the slice of life that matter. O'Casey was no dramatist of ideas; in spite of his previous interest in socialism and nationalism he does not have any didactic or intellectual purpose in his early plays. 'A dramatist is one thing,' he wrote, 'a revolutionist another, one looking at life in the form of individuals, the other as part of the collective urge and forward thrust of man.' He is content to allow the implications of the ideas held by his characters to emerge through the dramatic context and the conflict between the characters. Thus the waste of young lives is not attacked directly, but through showing the grief of two mothers who have lost their sons. The degree to which the ordinary citizen should be involved in politics is considered through the argument between Boyle and Juno. The audience is left to draw its own conclusions. It is given to a disturbed and hysterical youth to stress the emphasis on principles; although he is implicated to the point of being responsible for the death of a comrade, he has little real understanding of what he or the factions in Ireland are attempting to achieve. Similarly, Mary appears initially as a girl of principle but ultimately fails to assess the characters of the two men connected with her, or the implications of her actions in her love for Bentham. Again, no moral judgements are made. The audience can side with Boyle and Johnny in their attitude to Mary, or with Juno. Perhaps that is why there were no riots at the performances of *Juno and the Paycock* as there were at those of *The Plough and the Stars*. Another reason may have been the humour in the play. There is little point in trying to assign it the category of comedy or tragedy; it contains something of both. Shakespeare was an important influence on O'Casey, and he never attempted to exclude comedy from his tragedies.

Yet the comparison is misleading; at least in Shakespeare we can say with some confidence what is comic and what is tragic, even though there is an intermingling of characters from both sides. In O'Casey this is not possible, for the same characters are sometimes comic, sometimes tragic. Juno may be predominantly a tragic heroine; her husband, who has the larger part, is emphatically not. *Romeo and Juliet* would cease to be a tragedy if Romeo were a boastful, clowning drunkard. James Agate, in a review of the first London performance of *Juno and the Paycock*, wrote that it is 'as much a tragedy as *Macbeth*, but it is a tragedy taking place in the porter's family'. He notes 'that the tragic element in it occupies at the most some twenty minutes and that for the remaining two hours and a half the piece is given up to gorgeous and incredible fooling'. Twenty minutes of 'tragic element' does not constitute a tragedy.

The power of the play lies not in its plot or its theme, but in its humour. There is humour of characterization shown in Boyle and Joxer, sometimes in Juno, and in Maisie Madigan. There is humour of language springing from character, as in the grandiloquent use of word, phrase or quotation. There are the malapropisms of Maisie Madigan. There is the incongruous reference when Boyle describes the grumbling Juno as Deirdre of the Sorrows, or the drunken Joxer quotes Sir Walter Scott's lines on patriotism. There is the grimly humorous irony of Juno's comments on the principles and actions of those about her. When the play was performed at the Abbey Theatre the comedy was exploited to the full. Boyle and Joxer provide splendid opportunities for actors to exploit the comic potentialities of the roles.

There is some satire, notably in the sudden class-consciousness shown by Boyle when he hears about the Will. Bentham is satirized as a rising young man devoid of any trace of humanity. The difference between political concern for the welfare of humanity and the inability to love and support the individual in trouble is attacked in Jerry Devine.

The political background is an important theme. The room where the action takes place is an island in a very stormy world; a son can be removed to be shot, a bullet in the face may be the result of looking out of the window.

The Shadow of a Gunman had as its background the war against the British government and the 'Black and Tans'. As a result of this conflict a Home Rule Bill was passed in 1920, dividing Ireland into two. The bitterness caused by the struggle for independence proved fatal to the success of this Bill. The measure was unacceptable to the men in the North who wished to have their own local Parliament and to be represented in the British Parliament. In 1921 the Irish leaders formed a Treaty with the British government, setting up the Irish Free State, which consisted of three provinces, Munster, Leinster and Connaught, with a parliament at Dublin and Dominion status. Ulster was to remain separate. Many Irish urged the setting up of a Republic that was completely independent of Great Britain. These extremists, or 'Diehards', refused to accept such a Treaty. Civil war broke out between the two Irish parties, in which the Republicans were defeated by the Government and the Irish Free State came into being. It is against the background of this civil war that *Juno and the Paycock* takes place.

The break-up of the Irish nationalist movement in civil war is mirrored by the break-up of the family. The state of chaos exists inside the family and outside in the world. The strength of O'Casey is revealed in the interrelationship.

The Socialist theme through Mary and Jerry is dealt with less confidently. Mary's situation and betrayal have a touch of Victorian melodrama discordant with the moral realism of the rest of the play. The conclusion, 'Your humanity is just as narrow as the humanity of the others', disappoints with its air of contrivance.

The plot moves through a series of emotional scenes rather than in a well-ordered progression. The seeds of the final breakup are sown in the nature of the characters at the beginning of the play. It is inevitable that the marriage between Boyle and Juno will break, that misfortune will come to Mary, that violence will claim Johnny, and that Boyle and Joxer will drink to the very end. *Juno and the Paycock* is the sum of its individual scenes and its characters – all are vital and memorable.

Style

Sean O'Casey was brought up in a world far removed from the intensive training of school and university that conditions the style and outlook of the formally educated author. The literary influences to which he was subjected were heightened because they represented a burning need, the satisfying of a natural curiosity, and an insight into a far wider world. The chief dramatic influences were Shakespeare, the contemporary and popular dramatist Dion Boucicault, his mother's Bible-reading, and all the second-hand books he could lay his hands on; a further vital influence was that of impassioned socialist oratory.

It was, perhaps, inevitable that his early plays should be set in and conditioned by the slum tenement background in which he had grown up, and in which he was still living when he wrote them. In using this setting, and in his approach to it, he was ahead of his time, although his were not, of course, the first realistic plays. It is accidental, rather than historically significant, that he was an early exponent of urban realist drama. In fact, he could write no other. In the beginning he used only the setting and language with which he was familiar, and later he had no desire, save in the case of two plays, to relinquish his own Irish background.

Like Synge, another Abbey dramatist who had earlier used Irish peasant life as the setting for his plays, O'Casey transmuted what he found and knew through his imagination and poetic insight into a work of universal and permanent import. There is, however, one revealing difference between Synge and O'Casey: Synge was brought up in a middle-class environment and had a background of university education and cosmopolitan experience of life and literature; he observed the peasant life and speech, recording what he heard in notebooks. He witnessed it from the outside — with interest, insight, and sympathy – but still from the outside. O'Casey, on the other hand, was a product of the Dublin slum scene; he was of it and in it.

Synge's imagination led to a vivid creation of the peasant background and speech – O'Casey's to an intensification of his own life and background. Synge used peasant speech as a basis for the creation of characters whose purpose was to convince in the theatre: 'Those characters only exist on the Abbey stage', one friend asserted. So it is with O'Casey. He takes the life and background of a slum dweller and, by sheer imagination and style, transforms it into a fine dramatic interpretation.

All his characters are larger than life and infinitely more energetic. O'Casey claimed that he discarded his theories and worked out the characters in writing his early plays; they are all close to caricature: the drunkard, the deserted girl, the hard-working, earnest wife, the sycophantic drunk, the confused nationalist, the would-be socially superior young man. Despite this, the major characters have conflicting sides to their personalities and a depth and richness that make them vivid and convincing human beings.

The differences in speech-style among the characters emphasize their individual humanity. Boyle's oratorical flourishes are contrasted with Juno's simple expressions. Joxer's catchword 'darling' begins as caricature, but when it is added to a veritable battery of quotations from literature, it ceases to be an artificial dramatic device and becomes a form of rich humour. Note, too, O'Casey's rendering of Irish pronunciation by his spelling of such words as 'murder' ('murther') 'trench' ('thrench') etc.

Sometimes the sudden quirks of character have a grotesque quality. Bentham is a prig. Prigs are usually dull. His introduction of the concepts of Theosophy, Vedas, Prawna and Yogi into this background is pedantic and inappropriate, yet its very ridiculousness adds another dimension to the play, and, in the reactions of the other characters, provides greater insight into their personalities and creates a splendidly humorous situation.

Nothing evokes so effectively the feel and texture of a period as its popular songs. Undoubtedly their use has 'dated' this play and, for the purist, that may be a condemnation of this practice. However, when the authentic re-creation of an era is called for they have a legitimate – and usually attractive – place.

The prevailing impact made by the overall style of *Juno and the Paycock* is one of richness, mainly achieved in the rhythmic, oratorical flourishes in the speeches of Boyle, in the wailings of Mrs Tancred: 'O blessed Virgin, where were you when me darlin' son was riddled with bullets, when me darlin' son was riddled with bullets! ... Sacred Heart of the Crucified Jesus, take away our hearts o' stone ... an' give us hearts o' flesh! ... Take away this murdherin' hate ... an' give us Thine own eternal love!' (p.46).

The conscious nature of O'Casey's dramatic technique can be seen in the final speech of Mrs Boyle, which is a close parallel to this: 'Blessed Virgin, where were you when me darlin' son was riddled with bullets, when me darlin' son was riddled with bullets? Sacred Heart o' Jesus, take away our hearts o' stone, and give us hearts o' flesh! Take away this murdherin' hate, an' give us Thine own eternal love!' (p.72).

This consummate artistry belongs to the world of poetry rather than to the drama of realism. Notice, too, the use of the catchword 'darling', on quite another level to that on which it is used by Joxer.

Boyle's final reference to 'a terrible state o' chassis' is used five times during the play. A statement which begins as a throwaway grumble designed only to arouse laughter comes to sum up, incongruously enough in the mouth of Boyle, the prevailing mood and the idea of the play.

The style matches the atmosphere; the material is not intellectually ordered; the ideas are part of the pattern of life that is presented. Feelings are more important than ideas.

Intellectual conclusions may be implicit in the feelings and the events, but they are never made explicit as an end in themselves. O'Casey admired Shaw enormously, but his own dramatic approach is very different; Shaw's pre-eminence of intellectual excitement and the subordination of life to ideas was a complete contrast to O'Casey's emphasis on life and emotion.

The use of symbolism is part of the poetic approach. The removal of the furniture in the third Act symbolizes the final break-up of the Boyle family; the gramophone symbolizes the artificial good fellowship that Boyle is attempting to create, especially against the background of Mrs Tancred's speech.

If the choice of word is often poetic, it can also be commonplace. Yet this, like the popular songs, can be a revelation of character. When Boyle refers to 'that lovely daughter o' mine', he is using words that are only shallowly sentimental, but when they are set against the background of his words on her pregnancy and the fact that Juno and Mary have left him, they have a second, ironic meaning.

General questions and sample answer in note form

1 '*Juno and the Paycock* is neither comedy nor tragedy.' Discuss.

2 Describe the impact the Irish troubles have on the play.

3 Contrast the relationships Mary has with Charles Bentham and Jerry Devine.

4 Describe the part played by the friendship between Boyle and Joxer.

5 Is Boyle a likeable or a contemptible rogue, or perhaps something of both?

6 'Mrs Madigan serves as a foil to the nobility of Juno.' How far is this true?

7 Describe the part played by popular songs in *Juno and the Paycock*.

8 How far does the use of language reveal character in the play?

9 What part does violence play? Give some indication of O'Casey's attitude towards it.

10 A dramatist sometimes identifies himself closely with one or several characters. Assess how far O'Casey is identified with the characters in *Juno and the Paycock*.

11 The style is an important feature in the creation of an Irish atmosphere. Describe the qualities of style that contribute to this.

12 '*Juno and the Paycock* is the study of the break-up of a family.' Is this a valid description of the play?

13 '*Juno and the Paycock* is an affirmation of life in the constant presence of death.' Discuss.

14 How far is humour a reason for the play's success?

15 An Irish play written for the Irish by an Irishman: why does the play appeal to English audiences?

Suggested notes for essay answer to question 1

Introduction – clear definitions of comedy and tragedy – then brief summary of main action of *Juno* – interaction of characters – setting – period – 'troubles' – any other relevant material *briefly* here.

The nature of the comedy in the play – verbal (include something here on dialect) – visual – some farce, techniques of comedy employed by O'Casey – dramatic irony – overhearing etc.

The comic interaction involving Boyle and Joxer – Mrs Madigan – Juno and her verbal power; then perhaps exits and entrances – almost knockabout sequences – the use of the sudden and unexpected.

Links with song and Joxer's rhymes – overtones of menace – the focus on Johnny (outside events) and on Mary (the tragedy of her pregnancy). Senses of social deprivation – the waste of Boyle – the gradual reduction (though she does not give up) of Juno.

Atmosphere of menace, fear – trickery – deception – Bentham and Johnny; the personal tragedy of Mrs Tancred, the one typical of the many; the personal tragedy of Johnny and the Boyle family; inadequacy of religion (perhaps more – the influence of religion).

Conclusion – the authorial overtones in the text – emphasis on deprivation – being caught in a place and in time – hopelessness of situation, laughter grim with the sense of nemesis – comedy and tragedy *but* balance of Act III towards the latter.

Note: Quote from the play. Any of the paragraphs above may be extended to follow the argument.

Further reading

Sean Eileen O'Casey, edited by J. C. Trewin (Macmillan)
Sean O'Casey W. A. Armstrong (Longman)
Modern Judgements: Sean O'Casey and his World David Krause (Thames & Hudson)
Sean O'Casey edited by Ronald Ayling (Macmillan)

Brodie's Notes

D. H. Lawrence	**The Rainbow**
D. H. Lawrence	**Sons and Lovers**
D. H. Lawrence	**Women in Love**
Harper Lee	**To Kill a Mockingbird**
Laurie Lee	**Cider with Rosie**
Christopher Marlowe	**Dr Faustus**
Arthur Miller	**The Crucible**
Arthur Miller	**Death of a Salesman**
John Milton	**Paradise Lost**
Robert C. O'Brien	**Z for Zachariah**
Sean O'Casey	**Juno and the Paycock**
George Orwell	**Animal Farm**
George Orwell	**1984**
J. B. Priestley	**An Inspector Calls**
J. D. Salinger	**The Catcher in the Rye**
William Shakespeare	**Antony and Cleopatra**
William Shakespeare	**As You Like It**
William Shakespeare	**Hamlet**
William Shakespeare	**Henry IV Part I**
William Shakespeare	**Julius Caesar**
William Shakespeare	**King Lear**
William Shakespeare	**Macbeth**
William Shakespeare	**Measure for Measure**
William Shakespeare	**The Merchant of Venice**
William Shakespeare	**A Midsummer Night's Dream**
William Shakespeare	**Much Ado about Nothing**
William Shakespeare	**Othello**
William Shakespeare	**Richard II**
William Shakespeare	**Romeo and Juliet**
William Shakespeare	**The Tempest**
William Shakespeare	**Twelfth Night**
George Bernard Shaw	**Pygmalion**
Alan Sillitoe	**Selected Fiction**
John Steinbeck	**Of Mice and Men** and **The Pearl**
Jonathan Swift	**Gulliver's Travels**
Dylan Thomas	**Under Milk Wood**
Alice Walker	**The Color Purple**
W. B. Yeats	**Selected Poetry**

ENGLISH COURSEWORK BOOKS

Terri Apter	**Women and Society**
Kevin Dowling	**Drama and Poetry**
Philip Gooden	**Conflict**
Philip Gooden	**Science Fiction**
Margaret K. Gray	**Modern Drama**
Graham Handley	**Modern Poetry**
Graham Handley	**Prose**
Graham Handley	**Childhood and Adolescence**
R. J. Sims	**The Short Story**